AMAZING SCIENCE

Temperature

Heating Up and Cooling Down

Written by Darlene R. Stille

Illustrated by Sheree Boyd

Special thanks to our advisers for their expertise:

Paul Ohmann, Ph.D., Assistant Professor of Physics
University of St. Thomas, St. Paul, Minnesota

Susan Kesselring, M.A., Literacy Educator
Rosemount-Apple Valley-Eagan (Minnesota) School District

PICTURE WINDOW BOOKS
MINNEAPOLIS, MINNESOTA

T0053036

Managing Editor: Bob Temple
Creative Director: Terri Foley
Editor: Nadia Higgins
Editorial Adviser: Andrea Cascardi
Copy Editor: Laurie Kahn
Designer: John Moldstad
Page production: Picture Window Books
The illustrations in this book were prepared digitally.

Picture Window Books
1710 Roe Crest Drive
North Mankato, MN 56003
www.capstonepub.com

Library of Congress Cataloging-in-Publication Data
Stille, Darlene R.
Temperature : heating up and cooling down /
written by Darlene Stille ; illustrated by Sheree Boyd.
v. cm. — (Amazing science)
Includes bibliographical references and index.
Contents: Is it hot or cold?—Measuring temperature—
Where heat comes from—How things get hot or cold—
Staying warm—Make a thermometer—Hot facts.
ISBN-13: 978-1-4048-0247-6 (hardcover)
ISBN-10: 1-4048-0247-9 (hardcover)
ISBN-13: 978-1-4048-0345-9 (softcover)
ISBN-10: 1-4048-0345-9 (softcover)
1. Temperature measurements—Juvenile literature.
2. Cold—Juvenile literature. 3. Heat—Juvenile literature.
[1. Temperature measurements. 2. Cold. 3. Heat.]
I. Boyd, Sheree, ill. II. Title. III. Series.
QC271.4 .S75 2004
536'.5—dc22
2003016464

Table of Contents

Is It Hot or Cold?

A gulp of milk. Frosty windowpanes.
Freshly baked cookies and a crackling fire.

FUN FACT

If you feel very cold, you might say, "I'm freezing!" On a hot summer day, you sometimes say, "It's boiling hot!" What other expressions do you use to talk about temperature?

Which of these things feels cool?
Which ones are cold, warm, or hot?
There are many words to describe
the temperature of things around you.

Measuring Temperature

How tall are you? A ruler can tell you.
What time is it? A clock can tell you.
How hot or cold is it? A thermometer
can tell you.

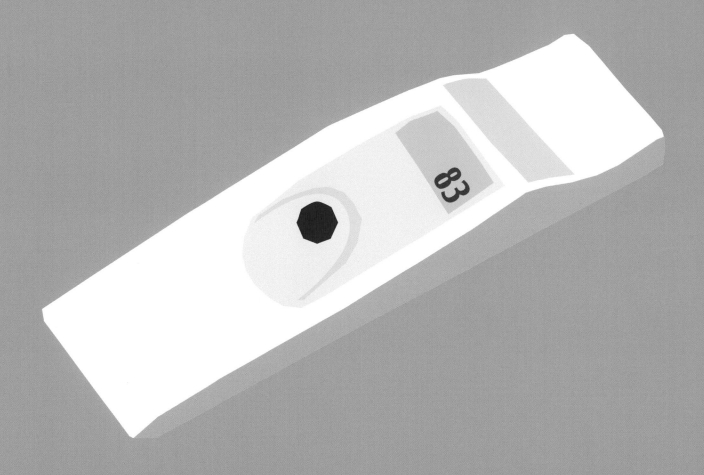

FUN FACT

There are different kinds of thermometers. Some have little windows
where the temperature shows. Some are dials like the face of a clock.
Some thermometers are glass tubes with liquid inside.

Rulers, clocks, and thermometers all have numbers that let you measure things. The numbers on a thermometer stand for degrees.

It is a sunny autumn day. It looks warm outside, but the air might be cold. Do you need a coat?

A thermometer can tell you. The thermometer tells you the air is 32 degrees Fahrenheit or 0 degrees Celsius. That's cold! You need a coat to keep you warm.

FUN FACT

There are two main systems for measuring temperature.
Most people in the United States use the Fahrenheit system.
Most people in the rest of the world use the Celsius system.

Where Heat Comes From

Things get hot because of heat. Heat is energy.

Heat energy comes from the sun. Heat energy comes from things that burn. Heat energy comes from electricity going through your oven.

Fun Fact

Temperature and heat are not the same thing.
Heat is energy that goes from one thing to another.
Temperature is a measurement of hot and cold.

A puppy feels warm and cuddly
because it gives off body heat.

The puppy's body burns food to make heat energy. Your body makes heat energy, too. Your body has a temperature of 98.6 degrees Fahrenheit or 37 degrees Celsius.

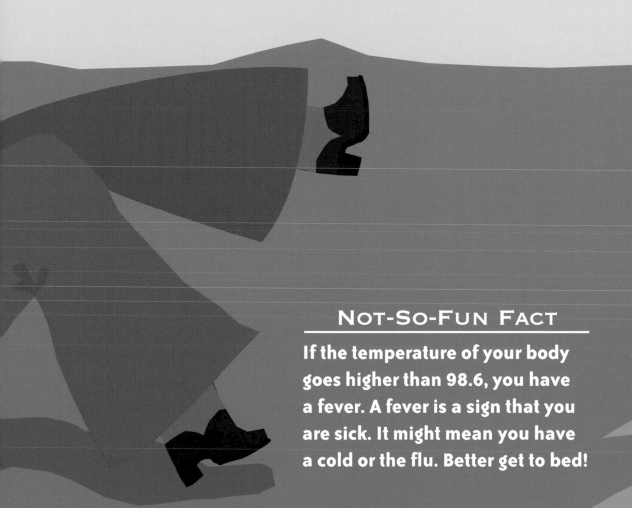

NOT-SO-FUN FACT

If the temperature of your body goes higher than 98.6, you have a fever. A fever is a sign that you are sick. It might mean you have a cold or the flu. Better get to bed!

How Things Get Hot or Cold

Heat is like a car that goes in only one direction. Heat always moves from warmer things into cooler things. Watch water boiling on a stove. Heat from the hot stove goes into the cool metal pot. Cool water touching the bottom of the pot gets hotter.

The hot water bubbles up to the top. Hot and cold water go around and around. Soon all the water is hot and boiling away.

FUN FACT

Things can also get hot without touching anything.
Rays of sunlight travel through space. The sunlight
reaches the earth and makes it warm.

Things get cold because heat goes away.

Put some warm cans of soda in a cooler with ice. It seems like the ice cools off the soda. Actually, the warm cans of soda heat up the ice.

Heat travels out of the warmer soda cans and into the cooler ice. *Losing* heat makes the soda cold.

Staying Warm

It's a cold night. A thick woolen blanket will help keep you warm. How? The blanket does not give off heat.

FUN FACT

Wool is good insulation because it does not let heat travel easily. Metals let heat travel easily through them. Blankets are never made of metal, and pans are never made of wool!

The blanket is insulation. It keeps your body heat from escaping into the cooler air around you. Your trapped body heat makes you feel warm. Sweet dreams!

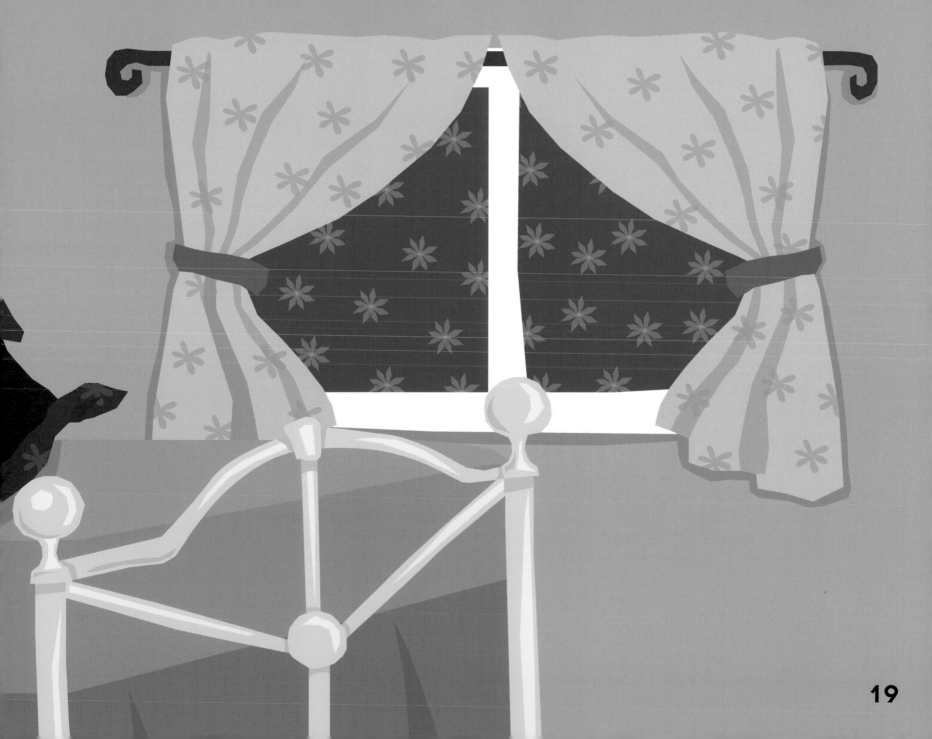

The early morning air is chilly. Your hands and nose feel cold. But soon the sun will come out and warm the day.

Temperatures are always changing. Heat is always moving. Now you know what makes things hot and cold.

Make a Thermometer

What you need:
a clear plastic bottle with a narrow neck
water
rubbing alcohol
food coloring
a clear plastic drinking straw
modeling clay

What you do:
1. Get an adult to help you.

2. Fill up the bottle one-fourth of the way with equal parts water and rubbing alcohol. Add two or three drops of food coloring. Put the cap back on the bottle. Gently shake the bottle until the coloring is mixed in.

3. Put the straw into the liquid—but don't let the straw touch the bottom of the bottle. (Do not drink the liquid. It could make you very sick!) Hold the straw in place at the neck of the bottle by pressing modeling clay around the top of it.

4. Wrap your hands around the bottle. What happens to the liquid in the straw? Now put the bottle in a warm, sunny place. Then try a cool, shady place. What happens to the liquid in the straw each time you move the bottle? Your thermometer works like a glass tube thermometer. The liquid inside goes up in the straw when the temperature gets warmer.

5. Be careful when you throw your homemade thermometer away. Pour all the liquid into a toilet or down a sink drain and rinse the bottle with water. Have an adult cut up the bottle so that no one can use it again.

Hot Facts

From Ice to Steam
Water turns to ice at 32 degrees Fahrenheit or 0 degrees Celsius. This temperature is called the freezing point of water. Water turns to steam at 212 degrees Fahrenheit or 100 degrees Celsius. This temperature is called the boiling point of water.

How Hot Can It Get?
No one knows how high temperatures can climb. The temperature at the center of the sun is 27 million degrees Fahrenheit or 15 million degrees Celsius. That's hot!

Brrrrr
Temperatures colder than zero on the Fahrenheit and Celsius scales have minus signs in front of them. Scientists think that nothing can get colder than -459.67 degrees Fahrenheit or -273.15 degrees Celsius. This temperature is called absolute zero.

Hot and Cold Spots
There are some places on the earth where the temperature is always warm. These places are near the equator, an imaginary line around the middle of the earth. There are some places where the temperature is always cold. These places are near the North and South Poles.

A Cozy House
Heat insulation is thick, fluffy stuff. Builders put it under the roof and inside the walls of a house. Heat cannot travel easily through insulation. When it is cold outside, insulation traps heat inside your house. Insulation saves energy by helping keep the inside of your house warm.

Glossary

Celsius—a system for measuring temperature that is used in most parts of the world
degree—a unit for measuring temperature
Fahrenheit—a system for measuring temperature that is used in the United States
heat—a kind of energy that makes things hot or warm
insulation—material that heat can't travel through very easily
thermometer—a tool for measuring temperature

To Learn More

At the Library

Auch, Alison. *That's Hot!* Minneapolis, Minn.: Compass Point Books, 2002.

Gardner, Robert. *Really Hot Science Projects with Temperature: How Hot Is It? How Cold Is It?* Berkeley Heights, N.J.: Enslow Publishers, 2003.

Granowsky, Alvin. *Hot and Cold.* Brookfield, Conn.: Copper Beech Books, 2001.

Martin, Elena. *Hot or Cold?* Mankato, Minn.: Yellow Umbrella Books, 2003.

Royston, Angela. *Hot and Cold.* Chicago: Heinemann Library, 2002.

On the Web

Fact Hound offers a safe, fun way to find Web sites related to this book. All of the sites on Fact Hound have been researched by our staff.
http://www.facthound.com

1. Visit the Fact Hound home page.
2. Enter a search word related to this book, or type in this special code: 1404802479.
3. Click the FETCH IT button.

Your trusty Fact Hound will fetch the best sites for you!

Index